Alanood is a seasoned Marketing and Communications professional that has taken on roles across global agencies and government entities. She was a driving force in launching landmark hotels, international events and TV shows. She has overseen regional accounts for local and international companies, most of which are household names. Alanood continues to play a role in the region's Marketing and Communications landscape; helping to bridge purpose and passion with consumption.

Alanood is also a member of Young Arab Leaders; educating and empowering the next generation of leaders in the Arab World by turning innovative business ideas into a reality.

In her free time, Alanood is with her family, friends and her little guy.

P.J.E.
PERFORMANCE INVOKING EQUATION

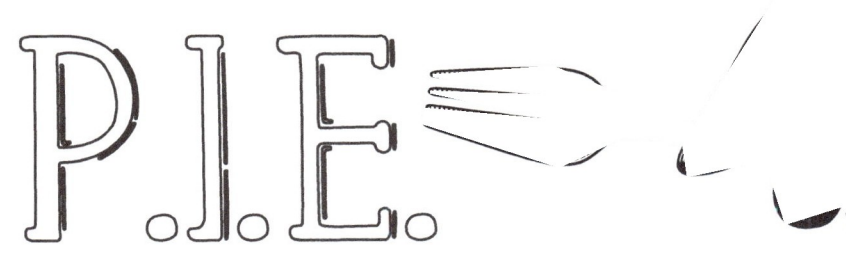

ALANOOD WALID

AUSTIN MACAULEY PUBLISHERS™
LONDON * CAMBRIDGE * NEW YORK * SHARJAH

Copyright © Alanood Walid (2021)

The right of **Alanood Walid** to be identified as author of this work has been asserted by the author in accordance with Federal Law No. (7) of UAE, Year 2002, Concerning Copyrights and Neighboring Rights.

All rights reserved. No part of this publication may be reproduced, stored in a retrieval system, or transmitted in any form or by any means, electronic, mechanical, photocopying, recording, or otherwise, without the prior permission of the publishers.

Any person who commits any unauthorized act in relation to this publication may be liable to legal prosecution and civil claims for damages.

The age group that matches the content of the books has been classified according to the age classification system issued by the National Media Council.

ISBN - 9789948259756 - (Paperback)
ISBN - 9789948259749 - (E-Book)

Age Classification: MC-10-01-8579551
Application Number: E

The age group that matches the content of the books has been classified according to the age classification system issued by the National Media Council.

First Published (2021)
AUSTIN MACAULEY PUBLISHERS FZE
Sharjah Publishing City
P.O Box [519201]
Sharjah, UAE

www.austinmacauley.ae
+971 655 95 202

To my darling boy…my catalyst…my cuddles…my being

Mom and Dad: Thank you for my existence.
Brothers and sister: Bless you always.
The Musketeers: Forever grateful.
Majed: Thank you for your existence.

La Hawla Wla Quwata Illa Billah

Brew some tea and bring your favorite fork, you're about to enjoy something truly delicious! Performance Invoking Equation, aka PIE, is your saving grace at work. It helps you develop the right mindset and gain the right tools and insight to help you constantly do a good job while still allowing you the time to perfect your craft and not get burned out.

PIE is a culmination of my own experiences and experiences of people close to me. We are some of the youngest global VPs, worked in agencies to launch some of the world's largest projects, brands, mingled with the famous, inspired many, patented technologies, painted walls, got on our knees and packed goodie bags before a big launch, the list goes on. Regardless of our upbringing, or lack of, we always chose to learn wherever we went. We chose to stay humble and stay hungry. We chose to find a way. We chose PIE.

PIE will speak to you. It's not targeted to any field, nationality, gender, it's targeted to you. You bought the book, you want some positive change and PIE will bring a slice or two of perspective.

Enjoy the read, and if you would like to reach out, I'm available on alanood@thepieplaybook.com

P.I.E: Performance Invoking Equation

A slice out of the corporate playbook to continuously deliver a winning formula without getting burned out

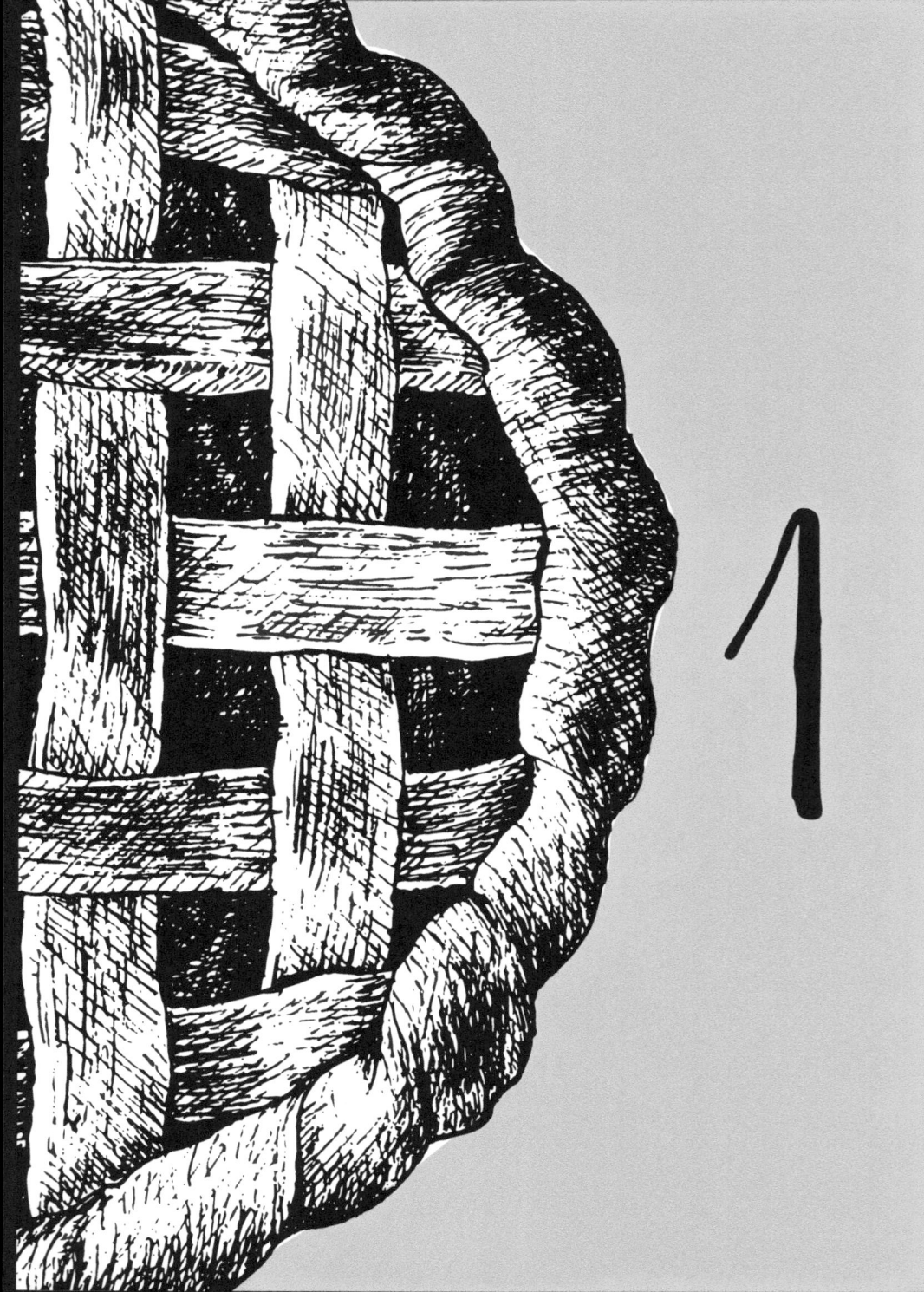

PIE

You're definitely wondering what PIE is and how it applies to the daily challenges we face at work.

Before we explain, let's set the scene...

and action!

You're at your desk, receiving an email a second being asked 'to do the needful' or a forward to FYA something you weren't looped into earlier. Basically, firefighting and reacting to people's requests while trying to complete tasks that have been planned and require a good amount of concentration. Now enters your boss in a panic state asking for 1,2,3. Suddenly you drop everything to do 1,2,3 and like a good employee you ask when this needs to be delivered. Your boss gives you a Dr. Evil smile, clinches their hands together as if summoning demons from below and says....................yesterday.

End scene

End life

Enter darkness and hopelessness

Enter anger and frustration

Enter *PIE!*

No, PIE is not the whipped cream delight that gets thrown at your boss's face. PIE is your panic button at those times when life gives you lemons and they're still ripe.

How are you supposed to make key lime pie with bitter lemons? Or with lemons in general? With PIE, you'll be able to give your boss that 1,2,3 with a little zest and a tiny squeeze that will satisfy their craving and leave you with energy to get on with YOUR priorities.

PIE takes those tasks that you know won't matter tomorrow but do matter to someone today and makes them edible; they probably won't get a Michelin star but you'll still get a 3 or 4 star review.

The inventor of Mind Mapping, Tony Buzan, said:

"The world isn't fast-paced, it's frenetic. People have to be managers of themselves. Time has been managing itself for 15 billion years; we have to manage ourselves in the context of time."

Our world is dynamic and there's never a day like the one before. Trying to constantly prepare yourself for the unknown is draining but once you're equipped with the right tools and the right mindset, you'll be able to navigate the corporate world and still make it home in time for dinner.

Ultimately, PIE is a mindset that you switch on when you have consciously measured the required outcome vs. the expected outcome and they are unbalanced.

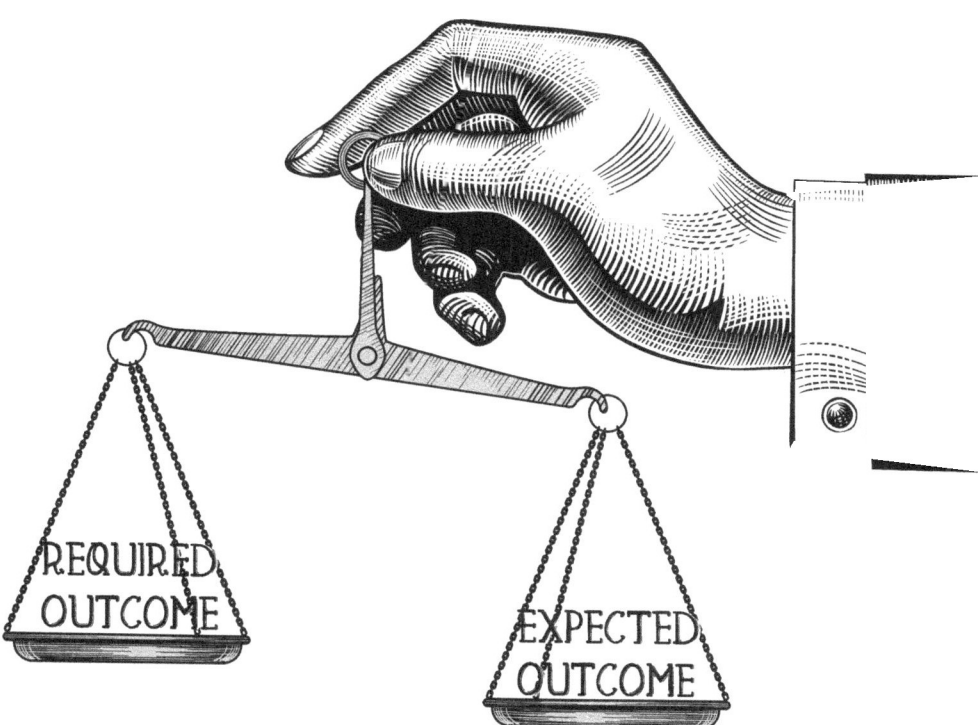

HOW DOES PIE WORK?

As we mentioned earlier, PIE is a mindset that you switch on to help clear your plate of urgent tasks. PIE is also built from years of hard work, networking and establishing a good brand around you. That brand is your badge of honor and the perception of others in your organization and elsewhere. It is what drives PIE. You would buy a cookie from Mrs. Fields or get a cake from Betty Crocker because you have established that they are good and consistent. Would you risk buying a generic brand? You might but not when you're in a hurry and need a sure thing.

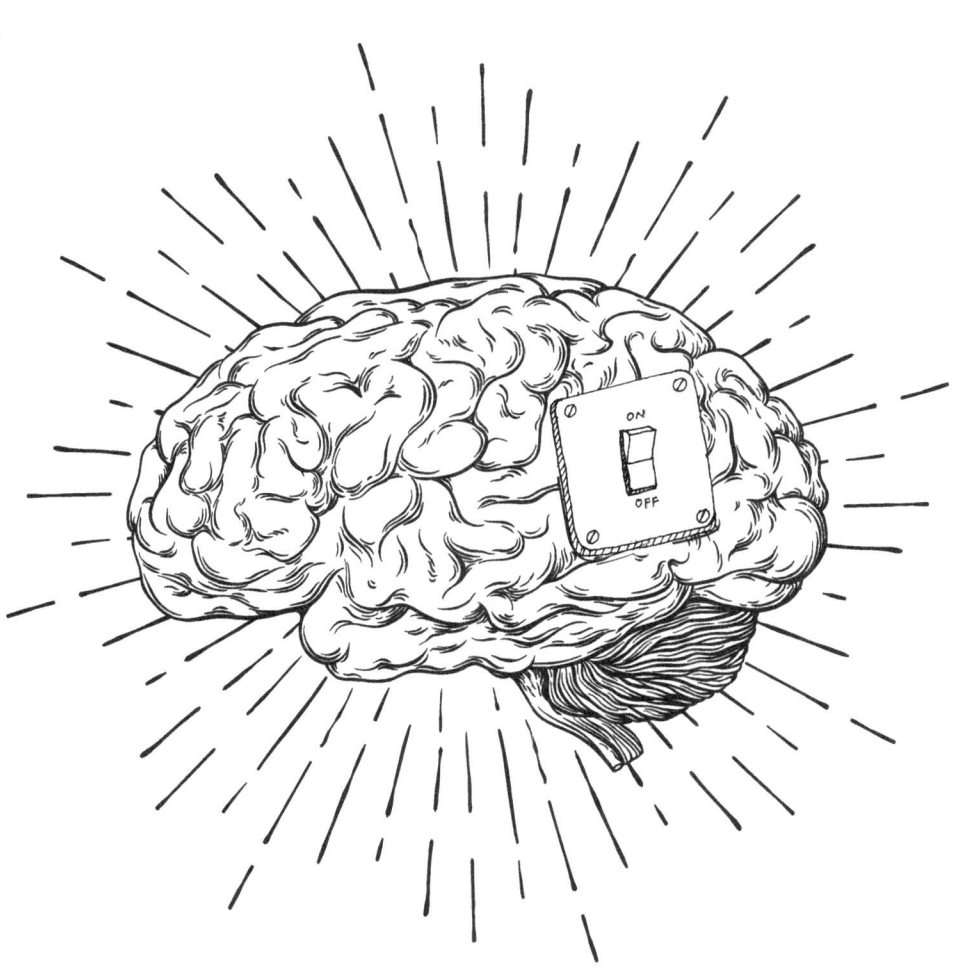

The PIE Maker

(aka you and we're calling you the PM from now on)

needs to be identified with specific qualities that an organization can trust and can enjoy. Once you've established yourself, you are able to be creative and see what works by understanding your stakeholders and tweaking your recipes to their satisfaction.

In this instance, we're speaking about the organization and the requestor.

The organization is what you produce, the requestor is the buyer.

Don't forget that PIE is meant to be a good product. Before Mrs. Fields commercialized her baking, she was a great baker and that's what a PM is. When you need to make something beautiful, delicate and divine, you will and you can. But remember, people don't want artisanal all the time, most of the time a good old-fashioned anything would do the job just fine. Understanding and accepting this will provide you with the energy to get on with your tasks, while still leaving room to perfect your craft, your signature and the reason people come to you in the first place.

Back to your brand. Your brand is nothing to take lightly. It is important to nurture and build it along the way. "Every advertisement should be thought of as a contribution to the complex symbol which is the brand image." The Father of Advertising and original Mad Man, David Ogilvy got it and has passed on his wisdom to you. Take it and run with it.

Throughout the Advertising industry, we have tried to humanize our products; personify an object. Why? Because it's in our innate nature to connect and find meaning. It's easier to do that when we are able to relate.

You, my fellow PM, need to be relatable. You need to know how to speak to people while maintaining your thoughts, values and direction.

WAYS TO BUILD AND MAINTAIN YOUR BRAND:

FIND YOUR NICHE

COMMUNICATE YOUR THOUGHTS

REPEAT

SHOW YOUR WORK

NUDGE, DON'T FUDGE

In no way whatsoever is PIE about lying, cheating, faking or fudging. keep those for the brown-nosed brownies! We are not in the corruption business and prefer to stay away, thank you!

We are not saying you won't fluff though. Everyone enjoys that airy fluffy cream you mix into the filling don't they? But with all that fluffiness and bounciness, Bakers still put in those key ingredients that make a pie a pie and PIE is no different. The core ingredients and some flavor notes (not all, you don't have all day!) are there just enough to be labelled a PIE.

Because of the circumstances, time limits and the general perception of quick turnaround projects not on our side, PIE-ing is almost always unique but our core stays true.

What's the corporate core?

Here you go!

Message:
craft your content wisely allowing to have an instant impact with a lasting impression.

Exploration:
take a moment to look at literature, speak to people, analyze data and round up a focus group if you can.

Relevance:
make it relevant to your audience and make sure the timing is right.

Inclusion:
PIE requires a general buy-in or 'heads up' to help minimize any negative reaction or major changes. People help make PIE but you are the music maker. You are the dreamer of dreams.

Target:
Always understand who you're baking for and if it's good, it goes.

Even in our acronyms, there is merit in everything we do.

THE CRAFT AND CRAFTSMAN

PIE can't be used by everyone; it takes a certain kind of person to be PIE-ing around. A PM has witnessed adversity; has thrown him or herself deep into seeking knowledge and understanding; and has probably been OCD at one time or another. A PM has done overnights at the ofice, the weekends and public holidays. They look at their computer more than they look at the faces of their loved ones. They've gone deep and they've survived! They crawl from the depths of the corporate gloom clinching the holy grail, the ultimate playbook, the secret recipe, the word...PIE!

PIE Makers have a decent IQ, high EQ and are Spiritually Intelligent. Dubbed in 1997 by Danah Zohar, the author of Rewiring the Corporate Brain, spiritual intelligence intertwines the parallels of IQ and EQ forming a commonality and reason behind them both.

Spiritual intelligence is not to be confused with religion or practicing religion, but SQ is the base of our entire purpose and is rooted in our morals and the faith we practice.

In the corporate world, SQ helps us see the bigger picture; play fair; not over stress on a task or situation; and keeps us grounded.

HOW TO UP YOUR SQ GAME?

- Meditate.
- Go beyond the ego.
- Ask yourself "Why" and answer "I don't know and that's okay".
- Forgive and love.
- Take notice. Our entire life is interconnected.

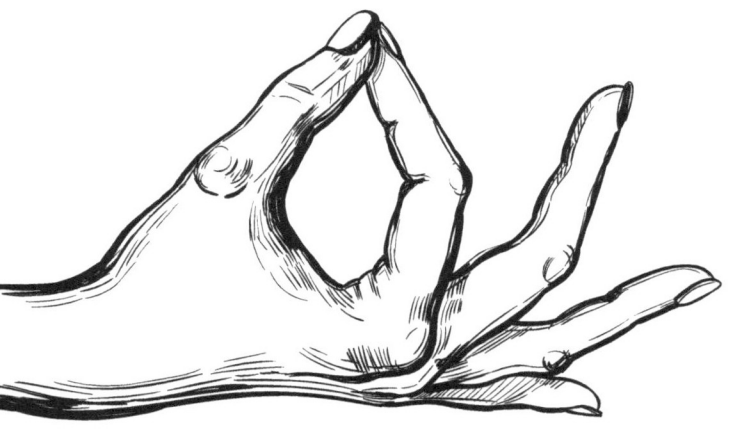

Taking notice is a big one. Have you noticed that most award-winning movies have plot twists where the protagonist pieces all those bits from their past, present and potential future and comes to the realization he is here because he was there? Yep...PIE.

Do not disregard any moment, any experience, any painting, statue or a blade of grass. You'd be surprised how and where inspiration comes from. The PM can see holistically while still adding in the details to make it personal...getting tingly inside? That's PIE.

Bryant McGill, a human potential thought leader and social entrepreneur said it well:

"You are the culmination of all that ever was. You are the highest point of the vast pyramid of history and of your own life."

To be qualified to PIE, you must have (or nurture) these traits:

CREDIBILITY

Charisma

HOLISTIC VIEW

SPONTANEITY

ABILITY TO REFRAME

Self-awareness

SELF-INTEREST

In his book 'Wealth of Nations,' the 18th Century philosopher and father of modern economics, Adam Smith, said: "It is not from the benevolence of the butcher, the brewer, or the baker that we expect our dinner, but from their regard to their own interest. We address ourselves not to their humanity but to their self-love and never talk to them of our necessities but of their advantages."

Smith explains that people naturally work towards their self-interest and while the receiver is working towards the same, the good/product must meet the need the of the buyer in order to have a mutually beneficial outcome. While 'self-interest' sounds 'selfish' it is not. On the contrary, self-interest leads to the benefits of many because you are able to give what is needed while still having enough time and energy to focus on what is important to you. The receiver gets what he needed for fulfilling his or her self-interest. Self-interest spurs movement and ultimately increases 'smart' production. Self-interest also reminds you that you are important and so is your health and wellbeing. And it gives you the drive when some things just can't wait and we need to buckle up and get on with it.

But will driving at 90 mph on the express tollway be as uplifting as driving on the scenic route with the top down and wind in your hair? No. They will both get you from A to B but you'll have less fun on the tollway and reach in a quarter of the time.

SELF-INTEREST CHECKLIST:

EAT AND HYDRATE — Have 3 square meals a day. Keep hydrated and a enjoy a little snack.

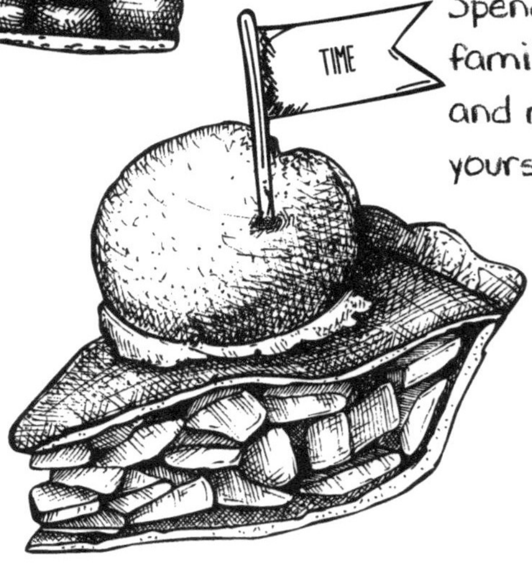

TIME — Spend time with family and friends and make time for yourself!

SLEEP WELL — Clock in a decent amount of sleep a night. However much it takes to feel well rested.

KEEP LEARNING — Keep learning. Read a book, the paper in the morning or take a LinkedIn course during your break. When you stop learning, you stop living, and when you stop living...well...you die done...done...done. ☹

WELLBEING — Take a brisk walk daily and pay attention to the details around you. Mental and physical health intertwine and you need both to thrive.

A LA MODE OR IN A JAR.
PECAN OR PLUM.
IT'S HOW YOU MAKE IT

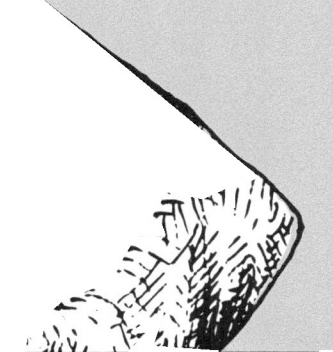

Pies have been morphed into an array of different looks and tastes. They've been pronged, deconstructed, doused in sauce, stuffed with chicken and mushrooms, holed up in jars, had a layer of cake put in between...the nerve! But all the while the main ingredients that make a pie recognizable are there: the crust, the filling, and the vanilla extract.

Life's PIE is just the same. The core ingredients are there - the 'assets', but the measurements vary depending on the scope of the job and the timeline. Your inner-self is wanting to do the best and do whatever it takes. You live by the mantra of 'you're only as good as your last battle'. Let's be real, you can settle for a tie in some battles. Give your soldiers a chance to rest and then go and win that war!

Let's take a moment and understand what our assets are.

Our assets are the ingredients we already have in the pantry. We've been working our whole lives perfecting that delicacy; that we've bought every ingredient, blender, non-stick pot known to man and used them probably once if we remembered to use them at all! Your assets can do the job and since they're there, use them! We can't even remember what we had for breakfast; do you think your manager is going to remember an image or template you had but never got to use because that project was 'put on the burner'? It goes without saying that these assets need to be relevant to the project and add value.

But always remember that whenever you are working on a project, envision what you may require a year or two on so you can have them ready. Hit as many of those metaphorically speaking birds with that stone!

HOW DO YOU PLAN FOR THE FUTURE?

- Read up on industry trends and see how much your company has applied them in the business.
- Gain a deep understanding for requestors' wants and needs through meaningful conversations and by taking notice.

- Have your projects include a 'legacy' plan so all the hard work put in them don't fizzle out in a short time. This will give you leverage when someone asks for a brand new campaign with similar objectives to something you have done before.

- Ask, Ask what's next. Ask what's new. Do not question, but enlighten yourself and others around you.

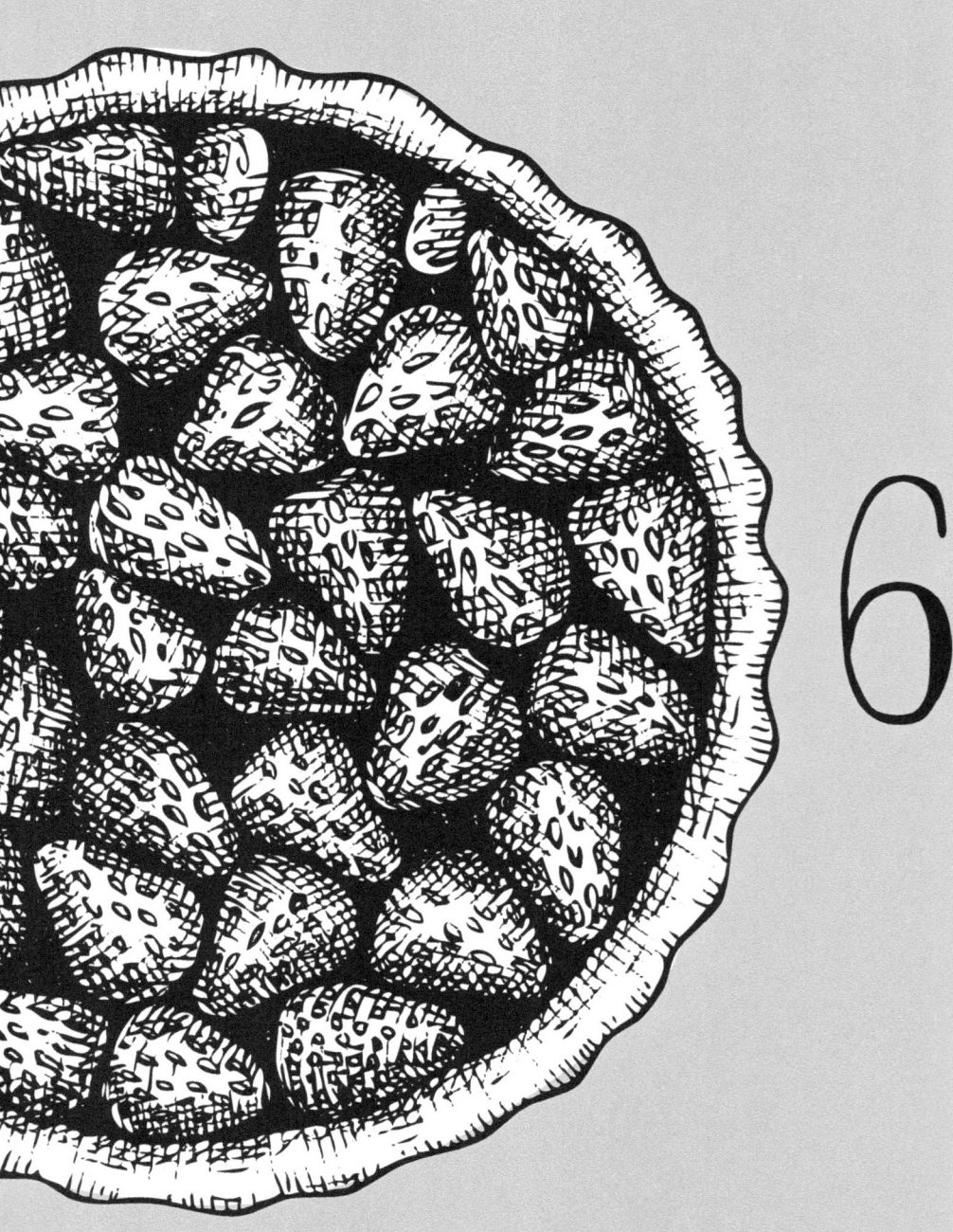

6

PIE IS NOT A PRIMARY FOOD BUT SERVES A PRIMARY FUNCTION

We'd all love to spend our day sitting in a bubble bath indulging in a slice of pie or around the kitchen table sharing a piece with family and friends but we can't.

Too much pie will make us lazy and gluttonous and eww.

Pie is your sweet treat after a marathon and at work, PIE needs to be used with caution so your quality of work stays high.

The purpose of PIE however serves a basic need we all have in our corporate surroundings: producing something someone wants but they don't know they want it. Feels a bit out of this world? It actually isn't. Many books have been written on the art of persuasion. They look at every angle, every nook and cranny, and every approach to subtly convince the receiver that this is what they need.

Late American broadcast journalist, Edward Murrow, said:
"To be persuasive, we must be believable; to be believable we must be credible; to be credible we must be truthful."

The concept of PIE is derived by this notion. Persuasion is a powerful tool and cannot be used by all. It takes someone like a PM to have it be effective since they possess the know-how to produce what's needed now and in the future.

How do you prepare for the future?

Perfect today.

With PIE, you will be able to predict tomorrow's needs through today's challenges.

Once you master this concept, you are always ready or at least you'll have a plan B and not be stuck between a rock and a wall. While we always say that we cannot predict tomorrow, we can have a general idea of needs and requirements.

Wants differ as they are subjective, but needs do not. Although, the wants will be the deciding factor when it comes to choosing who will work on the project.

Let's look at Maslow's Hierarchy of Needs. In any instance, the base of the pyramid is always shelter, food and clothes. Basic needs. In the corporate world, these don't differ. Understanding the nature of your audience and how they tend to react is a great way to help you prepare yourself for what's to come.

As you continue to go up the pyramid, you see that the needs become more subjective: belonging, self-esteem and self-actualization.

And this is where you, the brand you, comes into play.

MASLOW'S HIERARCHY OF NEEDS

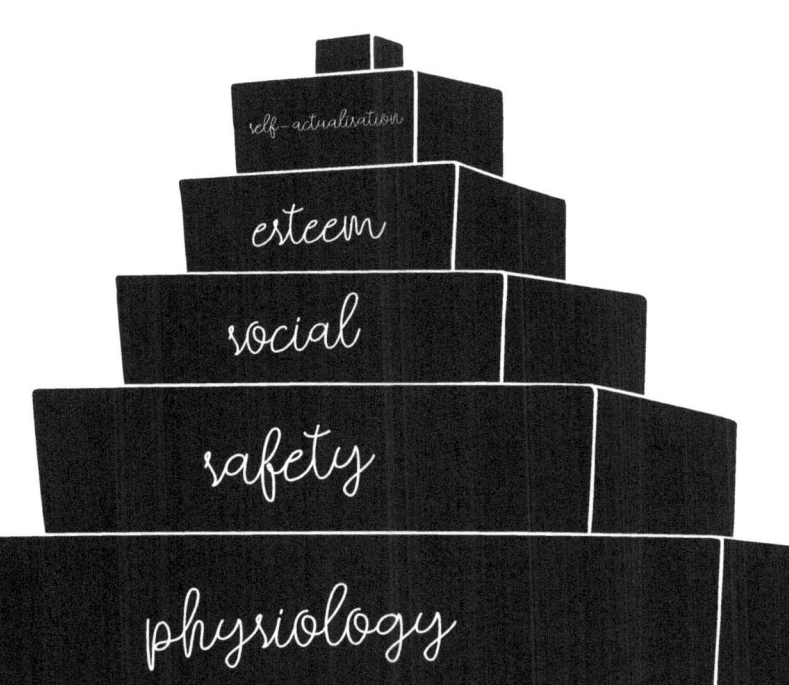

Like I've said before, PIE is a mindset but a PM is constantly honing in and re-tuning their craft. The teachings of PIE are adaptable and can scale up and scale down depending on the task at hand. Its flavor notes are a part of your overall recipe, your career. Tapping into the more subjective, while time and energy consuming, will be very rewarding as you gain loyalty and credibility amongst your peers and senior members of the organization.

THE BAKE OFF.
HOW TO PIE WITH OTHERS

You've heard of the saying "too many cooks spoil the broth" and if you've ever been in a situation when it was the contrary, please let me know. But by harnessing the power of PIE, you might end up with a fruit tart that everyone will enjoy. Collaboration and teamwork is necessary in organizations and cross-functioning departments.

While most PMs have OCD and would rather do things by themselves, you will need to learn how to bake with others and you'll be surprised with what you learn about yourself and others. Try to roughly understand every person in the group. Understand their role and understand a bit about their personality. Find their strengths, their flavor notes, and work with that to come up with a decent dish. Even if you feel you can do without their skills or they don't have any at all (highly improbable), give them a task that you might need to get off your plate but something with which they would feel accomplished. Checking the timer on the oven is mundane and boring, but too much time in the oven and your meal is burned. Get it?

Empower people. Whether with small tasks or big tasks, you will be able to encourage them to do more and in return you have shared wisdom and knowledge; marks of a leader, not just an employee. You might also want to consider them to present. They might need that pat on the back more than you (remember they came to you first for a reason) and PIE in general will never be your best work so why not share a slice or two.

Wondering how you manage the team? Through understanding their capabilities and by providing them a task they need to deliver. When people have purpose, passion is formed.

Let's meet our fellow bakers:

The wired one

We're going to start with the wired one because they can cause the most damage if not assigned to the right task. The wired ones generally tend to be pessimistic, angry and sarcastic in a resentful way. It's not their fault but it's how they're made. Try to understand that they usually have a lot of energy and frustration pent up inside them and have tried and failed to find a way to express themselves. If they're on your team, you can help them by making them release their energy.

How? Keeping them active. Get them moving, get them lifting boxes, or get them creating. Give them the tasks that require physical labor. It will help them release their energy and give them something to redirect their attention. Ensure that the task has something that needs to be delivered. Don't set them up on a wild goose chase. And of course, appreciate and recognize what they have delivered.

The intellect

These are your thinkers, your well-read people and your nerds. These kinds of people can help justify your idea and approach to the project. They can also provide a great deal of advice or point-of-view you might have missed. It goes without saying that everyone has something to offer and you should listen to what they have to say. How do you bring out the best in them? Let them do what they do best...read. Get them on the research, the planning, the data collecting and debating. Have them organize focus groups, develop surveys, and develop the methodology. Also, have them present the data because they will know how to back it up.

The social butterfly

These lovely creatures are your best tools when you need a majority buy-in. They are your eyes and ears in your organization and they are your own personal cheerleaders. Because of the nature of their personality and the connections they've already made at work, they have a good idea of their colleagues' way of thinking and can seed your idea during conversations.

They find ways to connect them with you in thought. In return, you get the acceptance of colleagues in a more subtle approach.

The butterflies also know how to flutter their way through the organization. In a project, they are best suited to be your project champion. Task them to relay information to the group and wider audience. Allow them to be the communicators, have them write scripts, do the PR, and engage with the audience.

These are a general snapshot of the different characters at an organization. A PM needs to understand that everyone is different. Like a pie, no two are the same. But also like a pie, you have to place the right ingredients with the right amount of seasoning and flavors to turn it into something good. If you misplace the ingredients, you will make a mess. The same goes with the bakers.

If put in the wrong positions, they won't deliver what you require. Assess and understand before you hand out a task and always remember that every person plays a vital role to the success of the project.

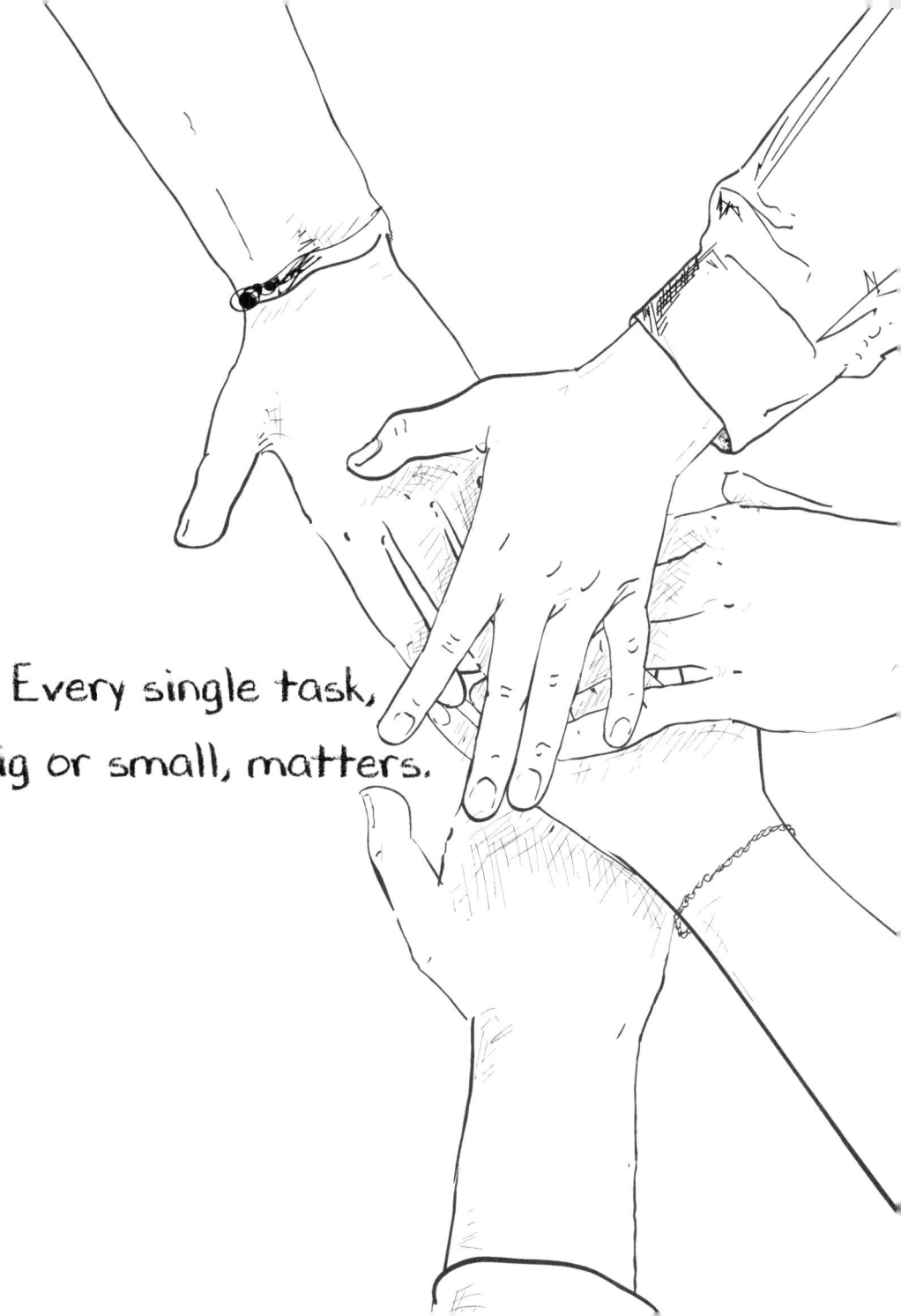

GO FORTH AND BAKE!

Dearest PM, you are now ready to go out and spice up your workplace.

You might have realized by now that you knew this stuff all along. You just didn't know how to express it; how to make sense of it; how to structure it.

What better way to understand it than with a good-old-fashioned food-based analogy?

And like our mathematical friend Pi, the formula for PIE is infinite.

Trouble's just a bubble
And the clouds will soon roll by
So let's have another cup o' coffee
And let's have another piece o' pie...

Irving Berlin

www.ingramcontent.com/pod-product-compliance
Lightning Source LLC
Chambersburg PA
CBHW040522220526
45473CB00013B/2949